Rebel Dove Poems

POET PASSENGER PIGEONS TAKEN OVER THE
WAY OF HORUS NOTIFY THEIR MESSAGES
ALONG THE PHARAONIC LINE.

Sylvia Horricks

 FriesenPress

One Printers Way
Altona, MB R0G 0B0
Canada

www.friesenpress.com

ISBN
978-1-03-910988-9 (Hardcover)
978-1-03-910987-2 (Paperback)
978-1-03-910989-6 (eBook)

1. Poetry, Subjects & Themes, Places

Distributed to the trade by The Ingram Book Company

DOVE CYCLE

ARIES 5

New Moon 9

First Quarter Moon 12

Half Moon 13

Third Quarter Moon 14

Full Moon 15

TAURUS 17

New Moon 19

First Quarter Moon 20

Half Moon 21

Third Quarter Moon 22

Full Moon 23

GEMINI 25

New Moon 27

First Quarter Moon 28

Half Moon 37

Third Quarter Moon 38

Full Moon 39

CANCER   41

New Moon   43

First Quarter Moon   44

Half Moon   45

Third Quarter Moon   47

Full Moon   48

LEO   51

New Moon   53

First Quarter Moon   54

Half Moon   55

Third Quarter Moon   56

Full Moon   57

VIRGO   59

New Moon   61

First Quarter Moon   62

Half Moon   63

Third Quarter Moon   64

Full Moon   65

LIBRA 67

New Moon 69

First Quarter Moon 70

Half Moon 72

Third Quarter Moon 73

Full Moon 74

SCORPIO 77

New Moon 79

First Quarter Moon 80

Half Moon 81

Third Quarter Moon 83

Full Moon 86

SAGITTARIUS 89

New Moon 91

First Quarter Moon 92

Half Moon 94

Third Quarter Moon 95

Full Moon 96

CAPRICORN 99

New Moon 101

First Quarter Moon 102

Half Moon 103

Third Quarter Moon 106

Full Moon 107

AQUARIUS 109

New Moon 111

First Quarter Moon 112

Half Moon 113

Third Quarter Moon 115

Full Moon 116

PISCES 119

New Moon 121

First Quarter Moon 122

Half Moon 123

Third Quarter Moon 125

Full Moon 128

GLOSSARY 131

The Egyptian god Thoth was credited with the invention of writing and of gifting this invention to the Egyptian people, a characteristic which makes the Egyptian god of knowledge and of scribes similar to Prometheus. According to myth, Thoth gave humanity a tool that allowed thoughts to be made concrete and enabled communication for strategic purposes.

The effects of Prometheus' gift to humanity include electricity and the resulting technology for accelerated communication. By enabling the use of the written word, Prometheus incited the use of technology for distant communication which has a place in inciting and enabling revolution.

During the 19th dynasty, watchtowers were constructed for military defense at strategically placed points along Egypt's north-eastern territorial confine. This confine was also a highway (for merchants travelling by land) and a trade route in use since the Old Kingdom, the Way of Horus. During the New Kingdom (1580-1080 B.C.E.) and Saite dynasty (664-525) these watchtowers surveyed land, river, and sea traffic and saw military campaigns leave Egypt for the Levant. Although the watchtowers were principally for defense, the ancient Egyptian army also attacked during combat.

Flocks of passenger pigeons kept at these watchtowers anticipated the telephone line and communication on an accelerated, instant network. Passenger pigeons kept the ancient Egyptian territory contained by enabling communication for strategic and defensive purposes between the easternmost watchtower at Rafah and the westernmost one at Tharu, present-day Qantara. The flight of passenger pigeons along a skyway corresponding to the Way of Horus centralized ancient Egypt by enabling written messages to be sent from watchtowers to Tanis—an important pharaonic city on the Tanitic branch of the Nile—and to Sais during the Saite period.

This book is a compilation of messages morphed into poems by the passenger pigeons who carried them from watchtowers on the Way of Horus to the pharaonic capital. Upon receiving what he thought was military communication, the pharaoh at Tanis would have instead found Rebel Dove Poems describing what the passenger pigeons had seen along the 350-kilometer skyline, corresponding to the Way of Horus. The rebel passenger pigeons had transformed the content of the messages into letters that are as much poems on observations of ancient Egypt as they are tweets to the inhabitants of this ancient territory, composed in flight.

The poems are similar to electronic-medium content for implicating power structures or inciting social change. Some poems reveal the whereabouts of stirring revolt, notable from a bird's-eye view, others narrate ancient Egyptian mythology. The Way of Horus was a trade route and thus a highway for cultural exchange between Egyptian, near Eastern, and East Mediterranean cultures during the Old and Middle Kingdoms, before the construction of the watchtowers. The poems describe different historical periods, as if the passenger pigeons could fluidly move between epochs during their flight.

Thoth is also the god of the moon. These passenger pigeons based their poems on the lunar phases in each astrological sign, to explain what they saw in flight during each moon phase. Each poem is based on circumstances created by the divinatory properties of the the new moon, first quarter moon, half moon, third quarter moon and full moon in each sign of the Greek astrological calendar. Given ancient Greek fascination with Egyptian antiquity during the Saite period, poems by passenger pigeons in ancient Egypt are organised according to the Greek astrological calendar.

The altered military messages acknowledge Thoth, as they are inspired by the moon phases, the feminine aspect of the night sky in continuous fluid mutation, in contrast to the sun and its enduring association with militarism. Writing, Thoth's gift to humanity, is used for revolution in a system for accelerated communication, the Way of Horus, by the ancient frontier's own passenger pigeons.

See Glossary

Sekhmet

Serqet

Death of Horus

Ma'at

Nephthys

Nut

Bastet

lotus

Maneros

Khem

ARIES

Off Penelope's loom the pattern was taken.
So was bargained Rhodopis up to the four-digits,
Red Cheeks.

Fear has four hands and its choice-weapon is strangling.
How does she pin all those eyes to the peacock?

"Don't learn to count" said Aesop in the dark,
"lest at tower, you be tasked,
before each dawn, to number stars."

From adjacent walls, two daddy longlegs spoke.
Mechanical insectoid march, traced on walls conjoining paths
that met at the corner, for a discussion
on some intricacies of Sekhmet's plague-menagerie.

Moths that before let to fly from lioness stables, are there tethered by Ati.
Rye-leapers that Nile, never rising, had supplied with copper knuckles.
Beetles, in their pageant, that make reverent mimesis of Voyaging Sun.
Serqet, healer come by grace here, with her hair all up in a scorpion bow.

The mystery to the subject of false-spiders' investigations,
I had made of it a slinkey
when the emptiness of our inherited toy box
was essential for our drum.

New Moon Aries

On a Lower Egypt rooftop one new spring moon,
three figures scribe-desk sat,
exalting battle records.

Cupbearer at captive's marble corner,
fearful, in shadows
and in plain sight,
resignation-watched them.

Watched the winners, peaceful captors,
in the new moon after-banquet victory hours.
Fell asleep standing at the edge of a dream
about anticipating dawn.

Cupbearer could not write
but dreamt that
in a Lower Egypt House of Books,
he pointed finger to empty air space
and counted.

A pair of every kind of moth
came to be a sphere
choreographed with oil flame at its center:
a sphere of seven interlocking
circle-dance, airborne circumferences.

Over Lower Egypt, over land, a dream: dark sea.
Fixed at angle-right to wave-pulse, ark as an oil lamp
swayed below every kind of dust-wing.

Scribe-desk kneeling before that same flame
and its moths flying circle dances
under harmonious cooperation trances,
Cup-bearer cut out a shape from papyrus records.
Pages had been accordion-folded.

Woven flax, a pattern-frieze of cut-outs,
left out on the clothesline limit.
Suspended there
until the heat of moths' trance-flame faded out the stains
acquired in pursuit of transcendence.

Now mind-to-hand discovering,
Cup-bearer spontaneously unfolded
a papyrus chain of both sides' shirts,
washed out,
chainmail was dissolving
at the anemic collars.

At the shoreline, so alone,
biting rocks in hunger.
Teeth indented hematite
so from rocks released in streams
latent iron.
Lost One saw how stone bleeds.
Red Ochre.

First Quarter Moon Aries

Furniture was swept from rooms,

potions and recipes inherited evaporated into their plans

as they took creativity from hands

and left there exaggerated, wall-tapping-fingers.

Now a mouse chasing its tail is the only cyclicity there.

Angels, the only company in transcendence.

From spring valley walked an escapist

up to destination: hilltop-autumn.

Wire on an heirloom bracelet cuts like blade

and, like a blade, releases iron to soil.

Half Moon   Aries

To circle this town, shadow step.

Physics of dark house to alley permits no other way to move.

Houses' night-time corners

keep Moon's new incubating light.

The night and its dream hours

gave two Duat-worthy shadow angels, solemn at their duty:

immunity of scorpion's poison and desert's bride, strife deep-auburn.

Met with Ma'at night's angels.

Regenerate deep ocean ink, strap on your feathers, Ma'at,

just to moult away your wings.

Shed your harmony-way, scales and skin.

Dead coils will fall circling round twelve poles, standing harp strings.

Those will have been your grace.

Ma'at, know that kneeling as a last resort will be nausea-inducing.

Resignation lace to bird-feet eye,

veil concealing the wailing faces of Nephthys.

Alighting hawks upturned their wings, fists up in agony.

Nut, sky-heavy, was there affirming the despair

that vultures flew circling.

Third Quarter Moon   Aries

Hooks of myrrh, crocheted as a rhythm to despair,
fringe the edges of the bitter etesian-carpet.

Winds' transposed prayer downstreams far into the heat,
to where lemon letter-drops
recount it all to combustion sunlight.

Someone's collecting scratched-out psalm-petal notes.
String up your paper truth-say leaves,
kingdom's conquered trees accept them.

Holy Spirit is on the copper scale set now exposed.
Insects strayed by their passing plague
subtract from it the mass of the vernacular.
It balances at a thousand solstice-combustion mothwings.

Full Moon   Aries

That's Sekhmet calculating.
Lady-paw fist to shapely Bastet-shoulder,
now she aims.
Projectile extension up-river flies.
Wings keep percussion time.

This, when the lotus looks to the Nile's mouths
and admits evident defeat.

This, when mutations were scratched in venom
throughout priests' gold seed-record scrolls.

This, when in one wind-blown room,
wings drawn to an abandoned harp in the corner,
flew up to each note-point in turn,
picked out *Maneros*: hymn on the strings.

Drink the new wheat and barley in the humiliated vines:
it is throat-burning Khem-chemical mead.
Read the letters in this dark green air disarmed;
they spell out Sekhmet's insect-aim.

See Glossary

Heliopolis
Bull's Graveyard

TAURUS

Tree nuts accessed at highest branches' reaches.
Their mimesis: chemicals to air, recruited from theater's deep mine
and to rock therein, technically applied.
Nut trees yielded precious premonitions: gems,
imitation-cut as almonds and exchange-gifted.

"Say, Wise King, my dear,
why so ready to blindfold your ruminations, resolving
at the service of such fools?"

"Because they love me
for it.
Welcome, my Queen."

New Moon

From the space between my teeth,

he recruited one scale with a knife.

Held it up to oil light.

Then the finned fish we ate reappeared, it jumped

from the empty plate,

water surface of river Euphrates.

Picking harp strings one by one,

solving riddles as we laughed at chimeras.

By magic, the harp played on.

Contemplating carved senet pieces,

he was pronouncing incantations.

A chili pepper held between two mouths,

stepping also on my hands,

cat's cradle played with a string of sapphires,

kissing the bipedal lion.

Smoke consuming peahen feathers,

nectar onto these decanted.

Ivory and wings in gold,

why so many steps up to the throne?

First Quarter Moon

One eye on the carved harp-ram closed,
eye opened again:
lapis lazuli winked at me.

The harp I did not know how to play.
Ram head turned towards the strings
and recited songs, note by note, for me.

The harp-ram walked. I followed
and melodies to the end sustained.
Mystic string marching band.

Rhinos linked to Suspended Cromlech stone

shifting, as rays in a circle

those stormy nights with rainfall.

When Pixie Speaker opened her umbrella,

then, as a standing triangle,

forecast a yield of bitter yellow flowers.

Abandoned riders' stables:

halfway house where mutilated unicorns convene

to telegraph-whisper,

as Job imagined,

to their harnessed sister-horses.

Code of electric signals,

clumsy sibling crushes said by dots and dashes.

Rhinos, hinged there in Wiltshire, declare their love

...

...

by lightning.

Third Quarter Moon   Taurus

All of faith's sacred Heliopolis bouquets

kaleidoscope away

from compass-point papyrus stem-axes.

So the seeds of poppies stray

way out to the Bulls' Graveyard.

So malachite lotus ash

goes past rows of potted incense trees,

forgetting all about the reeds,

beyond granite-enclosed Paradise.

Wish on quick creation's breath;

it is spreading, now, the temple's myrrh seeds.

This, all at the speed of a golden drop:

Re.

Full Moon   Taurus

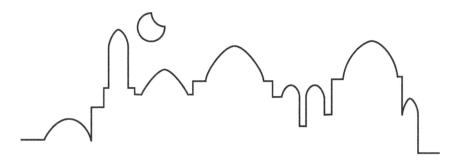

Full austral moon and walking birds,
for Tunis City journey, prayers.
Golden scales and prickly pears,
cacti for the pianist Lily.

See Glossary

Nile, Nile fisherman

Elephantine, landscape stone

Ra

Nile, low Nile

Nile, transformation by the Nile

Set

Bull's Graveyard

On

GEMINI

Conjunction Mimesis:

Remus remembered a poem – it was Latin, heard from wolves –
and picked it by the heart from the leftmost spoken word.

Soul recitation articulating motion to its hinges
reflected bilateral in mirrors
when his twin recited too, starting from the word most right.

Consistent pyrrhic rhythm, predictably maintained,
folds each line by latitude center from the sides.
Action conjoined actors when synchronicity was kind.

Their spoken pageant all through, in their handshake-upheld mirror,
twins incubated in one impression of embrace
they brotherly mimicked by rhyme.

New Moon

Starlight caught between three rocks:

a trap in speckled variations.

Sunlight finds its crevice home

with negative space confines traced by bitumen in stone,

replaces gone-stone, an out-cut obelisk.

Auburn crocodile as a minnow swims the mist.

Clouds like sheep forming herds,

souls of dinosaurs in birds.

Starlight still trapped between three rocks.

Dear Castor,

Instructions for the Underground:

Downstream.
Let out the sails to this lucid dream.

Feel your way over all the seas,
Ionian, Capri, and Adriatic –
there's Cagliari.
Four winds with their faces perceive:
they've got pollen grains for spices in their cheeks.

Cinnamon and saffron,
Eden's herbs in the Nile-fisher's net.
That's the Zephyr
and counter to the current, in the sail, that's Etesian breeze.

Exhale.
Upstream.

-Pollux

First Quarter Moon   Gemini

Dear Pollux,
Report from the Underground:

Chimeras have taken up residence on cement's highest rafters.
Ceiling-soil is an echo-board
that receives at times their hum,
that mixes earthquakes from their mono-pitched song.
With their sure wings folded,
wear-fragile their leather.

Biology is limited to the uses of a dead language.
Tedium reigns from the redundancy of hypotheses for the life sciences.
Out of boredom, geneticists have started making angels.
You were here, you will not remember
that you've tagged on the locks to their cages.

Feather pigments –
the game-table greens and the phosphorous russets –
are from deep-sea Renaissance medusae.

One, who can't fly, stand up yet,
claims to retaining your thoughts still in her lap.
With any luck, she'll soon find herself under the tutelage of Uriel.

Streetlamps here emit red light,
to direct such apprenticeships through initial stages.
The memoirs I'm composing by this invention,
I'm titling *Reason*.

First Quarter Moon

On request sent from *Schifanoia*,
one chimera was let out, back up Pu-Abi's narrow flight
of porous metal stairs.
The forward-leaning gate she climbed
was a gift of Gabriel.

Skyscraper-high, face winds of three seas witnessed
deep-ocean glowing big cat claws
down Moreau-indent shoulder-leather.

Feline sinuosity is derived in-lab from spirals.
Perfected lion tail showed its *5, 8, 13*-curve,
roof-high in lemon-scented darkness.

First Quarter Moon Gemini

From the opportunistic curiosity of an electric lamp's spirit –
Uriel refracted red beams
off a ruby in a cardboard box –
from light's wild aspect.

Structural rhythm was established
by gem's plurality of refracting surfaces.
Syllables caught in formulaic constancy of strophe
were by light, condensed to dust-dots.

At the *Hortus conclusus* of loss,
we have both drunk at the lion-faced well.
It holds bitter water when the moon is a crescent.

We wear honeycomb crowns.
On the left, below the lightwood table,
sits the ennea-point diadem in its spindly elegance.
On the room's afterthought of a milkmaid's chair,
kingly cabochons are placed where papal bees
made errors on the paths of their penta-walled construction.

First Quarter Moon   Gemini

At kettle's rim, a moth alighted.
Before it dove, Moth paused and waited,
instinct mastered its impulses,
as liquid fermented a cultured surface.

On tea-pond, Moth danced in performance of a Buddhist proverb.
Discovered by ripples, its wing-axis:
the range to which rotations opened.

Wings relished fly-stroke in the new environment,
as a butterfly-swimmer, affirming efficiently their presence.

Close behind there was a plague that followed:
pulsated biological wing-force at the window.

Air, forgive, I've here used in vain your aspects
and stamped with light your best angles.

                                        – Castor

Ibis, carry this blood note up
with flight that' s swift and sure.

Dear Castor,

Instructions for the Underground:

Sail on in this lucid dream.

Upstream from Elephantine,
granite fine print hides in landscape stone.

Against the emerald current,
search there all alone.

Commemoration Lighthouse
stands in tranquil trees.

Notice fire birds, Ra's timekeepers,
who melt wax by drips from mango leaves.

Cataract seven year low-Nile chronicles
absorb river's reflections, bouncing in prosperity-green.

See orcas by dozens, up, are rising.
Tides, their way, cross-horizontal.
Reindeer are Tundra-running.

Circle with Apollo's lyrical fish: the dolphins,
dive deep with whales,
swim the Ionian.

-Pollux

First Quarter Moon   Gemini

Dear Castor,

News from Islands:

Lychee trees, ash of flame-leaves
hold hands by harmonica-hum on high-petal breeze.
Close clasp by ends of chirr-chain to circle Quarry of Caves.

Lyre lines latent lie, to bee-combs transcribed,
under even films of amber:
lyrics layered asymmetrical up birds' reservoirs of honey.

Moths in plagues congregate at wing and shadow meeting.
Molts the macaw, over *opus* of the silkworm
while with zeal, mosquitos zip-anticipate disease.

Dancers-leaping swing up-steps, pep,
guided by directions they receive from cairns constructed at corners.

They cradle the Sun and ring-dance linked by light,
arms open wide, they keep stars all in sight.

-Pollux

First Quarter Moon

Dear Castor,

News from High Seas:

When vibrations on harp strings
that were pulled too tense
made glass splinter,
auburn ornamental fish thought
that she must have rebelled
from the inside of the glass of champagne.

Harpist, always indifferent to a chaotic scene,
aimlessly continued to pick out a melody
on the most tense of court instrument strings.
So went the night.

Sound skips rocks in a series of undulations:
a yellow slinky's coils hit the water
between the islands of the Nile's first cataract
and proceeded to the Dodecanese islands.
Then, by solar wind with the Auroras, to both poles.

Castor, there are pearls beneath the ice,
the kind that come in indigo and pastel green.
Know that there are divers:
ice-oceanids who find them.
Slender selkies, the kind with fins for hands, the green-haired kind.
Know that.

-Pollux

Dear Castor,

Instructions for the Underground:

So you keep clairaudient with angels?
The Earth Bird? Not material for Uriel.
You celebrate your capacity to reason, with the sphinx-makers?
You're self-referential. In competition, write me pages.
Envy the proximity I maintain to rhymester-muses.

Lie with underground neo-fauna, the flightless variety.
I can tell, you risk acquiring the stride of lab-chimera prisoners.

Interact with blood, paint, investigate blue.
Freedom – consult the detained about it:
the only philosophers trusted on the subject.

Buddhist proverb? Envy curiosity, given-us by life sciences.
Regret to not guard the seas, to not taste their pungent bitterness,
if you will not make a practice of my dreaming-formulae.

-Pollux

Half Moon   Gemini

At the gateway to the desert,

ages lasted combat and trial.

Focus meditation practice,

sunrise condemns to day's new sentence:

mountain-face isolation.

Transformation by the Nile,

tournaments and points rewarded,

fighter's love-obsession for the rival.

Fire fist to opponent's water shoulder fast-melded.

So energies seemed to be static.

To see the making of king and crown,

green and red supporters at Nile bank gathered.

Third Quarter Moon   Gemini

In combat, shadows go as boxers.
They're half giving, half receiving.
Fixed on circuit-walls of labyrinth, link passages' intricacy.
Step and sway, they alternate the yield and melding.

Shadows combat first with foot-left.
Than hinge, to shoulder-opponent swings shadow right-fist.

Improvised strategic dance,
opposite steps meld as corresponding pieces.
Ventriloquist, she speaks
to single dancer from the boxing match resulted,
Somersault into the dark,
psalm-advice from sealed-lips guided.

Superimposed stones, ovals for open land explaining,
balance at driftwood teetertotter center.
Method of honoring each rock's subtle equilibrium through feeling.
Work of four hands by intuition stone stories exploring.

Full Moon

I was fleeing with the Desert Lord
when he spoke Set words to me,

"Strings to a storm parachute, invisible
go to the Bull's Graveyard, past the last point
that the eye can see.
I'm running along by them.
This will mean we're free."

There was no better destination
to no place values gave.
Nowhere could have been better than what On could also be.

"Ring this calloused wrist, Artiodactyl, by hoof lead me falsely,
accessorising be.
Flower, with an earthquake gentle I'll uproot you,
taking nothing else with me."

See Glossary

Khepera

Bastet

Ma'at

Harpa-Khruti

Tefnut

Seshet

Set

Heru-Behutet

Grapes

Apelle

Tawaret

Min

Anubis

Bennu

CANCER

Clam, established fundamental, meets
with Earth-authority's regent-island.
Deep shell-creases firmly hold kelp-residue.
Once useful to keep watch on algae,
out of compulsion now retained, green as copper-rusted.

From the inside, shell top and narrow valve base,
on pigment stripes out-looking:
high tide beach exposes on metallic sand
ocean's lyrics, composed at nausea's eye the previous night.
Sky-suggestion is a narrow Khepera band.

New Moon

Each night on a Chicago city corner,

the Bengal cat called Madonna Bastet counts all her kittens' spots.

Cardboard-box litter of diamonds.

Then specters from the Children's House

come out to dance at hopscotch hour in a ring.

Each alley down they run is on a map of moats.

Urgent sneaker-gallop leaves rhythmic horseshoe tracks.

Rosie in the dying light, 'round cloister trees, 'round Gardens of Orange.

When they run strings of electric lights

down Castle's entrance-lines of columnar pines,

they are invoking Uriel.

At their court the jester spears another rat,

blood to the chess tile floor, alchemical death dance.

Flesh to sustain the hunters' day, their team of leopard cats.

The pheasant turns one wing up

as a street-discarded fan:

arch that fits the sun-ring's missing piece

in a wish-bone snap.

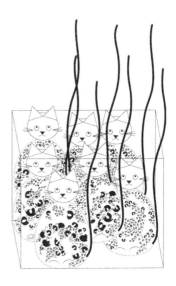

First Quarter Moon

Hands at the tips of Ma'at wings,
an oasis hammock's lift, quiet
by the shadow of starry cow, push to perceive.
Moon barge crescendo, palm post held
and drugged, to sail the Sky Way.

Choir of fireflies by open note up-columns lullaby,
swing to sleep, Harpa-
Khruti.
Books on his dreams, silent by Tefnut's lion tides,
go checked as lunar cargo.

Nothing's left of Poetess Fireflies',
strophe-echo at elephants' grave.
Though that night bugs, they say, in a choir sang-chemiluminescent:

Ma'at transcribed your dreams to beer 'n wings.
Tight scrolls in red profane they'll be receiving at the Book House.
Sleep this first-class-cabin night,
Seshet sent your dreams as cargo.

Half Moon   Cancer

Dear Set,

When in this Nile bath
as a hippo I submerge you, as a serpent you will be –
that's how I will have prepared you.

Came fire at its stolen state
to be framed in a sphere resplendent
with wings.

Came Heru-Behutet.
The navel sky battle, he started it.

Heru-Behutet waterways soon ran sweet with grapes.
Victoria home to his city came,
alighting multicolored.

On the dark lawn languid,
they consumed by bird pecks, mannerism, tooth and tongue
Apelles' sprigs of vine.

They deep purple devoured their still life, grapes from Mytilene.
And the scene Isis came to light with moth lamps, lunar powered.
The Dog-Star watched them be.

Half Moon

There is a place that Thoth has named,

it is only waiting

for your destructive presence, the inevitable.

Away as grapes,

these ink tears I'll erase downstream,

wail for the enslaved who cannot cry.

Away as iron ashes,

these crocodile scales I'll off-brush and up-skyway send.

Walk as a disk-winged, from the West Bank of the Nile, shining wild.

When as a hippo, moving river shadow,

I behold you good as new

walking from the West Bank of the Nile.

Love Tawaret

Au Fleece.
Beach glass wind chime, a mobile.
Held in fleece, woven metal,
one moment's tension, a split bottle.

Traced the upper numbers
of the conch shell's ridge, ascending.
A gloved finger glided the sharp turn ending.

On canal serene, an omen drum:
reef's waters breaking,
metronome for chimeras singing.

Indigo harp and violet cello
crushing foam on rock ice cubes.
Sound: a flicker from the yellow lighthouse.

Heard from map's third part edge,
a lethal song, yet *Meeresstille.*
Come home to Lido.

Full Moon   Cancer

From the kitchen's jade island-top,
Neptune paces the fishbowl.

Runs the first deer in the carpet,
birds who see her dare to circle.
Home Tree weeping, is abandoned,
menagerie is animated.

The olive connects-circular two sprigs:
from body tree, out a crown.
Animals talk, birds walk and caught in descent and fin-ascent,
fish circuit-swim *nymphéa* pools.

As a door-high statue, arch-entrance placed,
the speckled dove was speaking.
Doe, she-fawn is of mutable pelt,
new sunlight waxed in young spots as gold.

Set, as a leopard, with scars displayed as spots,
in a robe of light-red, bipedal-stalks Min's halls each dawn.

Full Moon   Cancer

Spring's season slip – granite-smoke tint
and Bastet wore her Mau-cat pelt as spotted silk,
robe-folded at the collar-neckline.

Pearl, the tear, chocolate-salt, by pendulum Bastet was swinging.
Time put down a 2/4-gallop-walk to metronome's chain-needle.
Sea-gem, at moment-counts of turn-around-stop,
Anubis eye-hit at trajectory-edges.

Bennu recounted what he saw at ray-ends of the circle-Sun.
Ibis scribe-folded wings sharp – a square, to listen.

See Glossary

Sekhmet

Bastet

Anubis, jackal-guide

Hu

Khem

Aat Sanctuary

Ma'at

Seti

Was

Leopard

LEO

Sekhmet resurrected sand cats when she desertified the land.
Eyes shaded, Bastet had painted on their bands.

Shoulder small, cupped by giant hand, a paw,
Bastet points sad ones
to crowd assembled under leadership of their jackal-guide.

Some hesitate, afraid of dogs.
"Your team are they," Queen Cat says.

Bastet blinks her eyes in approval as they go.

New Moon   Leo

Hu, Magic, Sia: fraternal trinity,
link day-arc's sky-points on the celestial circuit passage.
They go affirming last night's spoken Nile Delta vows,
with their cup-drinking, elbow-interlocking trick.

Validated utterance,
the lyrics of oar rowers' Sun Song,
take premonition wishes as cargo,
past the spheroids,
up sky to destination Evening.

River boat celebrates its Dawn-Dusk symmetry
only to decrescendo soon the light of day
and bring back fresh lotus, knife cut.
A piece of night-sky harvested in a bouquet.

Chance sightings of zodiac's menagerie,
shadow appearances seen running late,
at half past time of arrival.

Phaethon later feared those same star-conjunctions:
chela hinges, mobile far in the reaches of their range,
jaw-stars, than venom.

Noon day's hot light is already in your eyes,
yet desert's frigid night is still in your bones.
Seed pose at deck's tragic center point,
on the intersection of the Khem-crimson lines,
where Fortune, herself added to the crew, has got you.

First Quarter Moon   Leo

Cracked screen reflects high noon Sun
after sand-suicides are run.
Application for tracking Mars
prescribes red chili water rations.
Held immobile first,
spear pierces the ground,
exactitude refined by focus.

Fireflies refracting off embers
explain, by movement, Khem pattern circuits.
Austral dusk wind is dispersing
from concentric meditation flowers,
each *kyil khor* strand of tobacco
laid through investigation
into the nature of bonfire ease and solace.

Half Moon

Leo

The fire was four undulation-ribbons in smoke:

each one released moths of vapour.

A shadow dance ran 'round me in a circle:

memories of antelopes in a ring

alternating with light-footed shadows of hunters.

Third Quarter Moon   Leo

Aat Sanctuary, womb that incubated sibling trees:
sycamore, acacia.

That's where fireflies together rise to recognise
the mechanics of Ma'at.
There's a cataract that spouts a Nile vein, the mother place of iron.

That's where fields bleed at the valley confine
when they should be golden.
There's an angel who, by moulting, shows grey bone.

That's where Anubis with was scepter calm and even,
leads exemplary his flock.
There's a leopard whose spots spiral Milky Way along his slinking back.

That's where, like Seti, they pray to Set.
There's a girl who lighter-burned a red rose she'd received
as a silent sermon.
Aat Sanctuary.

Full Moon   Leo

One lioness come upon a fetal pose, paced around it out a square.

The two had absquatulated into the beyond predictably,

when they crossed paths

with timed precision subtle as an aura shifting from body in a step.

That lioness for the fetal pose she knew, turned grass over,

Amen,

dug a grave in the way of tribe and kin.

See Glossary

Tefnut

Qerti

Qebhet

Elephantine, elephant

Geb

VIRGO

Tefnut's shepherd flocks her lambs in generated yields.

At feeding directs them tri-part stable vortex through.

They compete at Qerti.

Then, on their momentum: thirsty strife,

Tefnut's shepherd sends them to open Milky Way.

Watching middle-river Qebhet, Thoth had that be observed:

a shape-changing circle-island,

morph in empathy for the elephant.

By Sothis Star, gardens on west island side

brought to stairway edges amem seeds, shape-shifting too.

Solid granite thighs shifted by the island's hip rotation.

Alabaster smiled, incense and sehi.

New Moon

Virgo

Between limbs in cow pose wind moves,

whispering to shells in the sand.

Austral breeze displaces lion paw prints.

Sun salutation is received by rising Sol time morning.

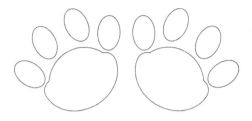

Here actions have no consequences.

First Quarter Moon   Virgo

Sail-triangle tips newsprint, nose down,
gives paper-wreck to floor-sea and with it cargo-dreams.

Play pirate ships passing wave peacefully *Ahoy*.
Sea-coins watch stowaway passengers,
heads' copper blushes rust-accretion – in envy of emeralds.
Caves echo with stories of *mind over treasure*.

Weed-dandelions watch herds, fields-over,
spear lions-entered, wear manes.

Half Moon

In my pocket is a drop,
piece of shore enclave in purification territory,
word in a language spoken by birds,
petrified petal worn smooth.

Drop in a pocket weighs like the sea
and buckles knees under as does sinking sand:
earth trickster
who plays on attachment to motherland.

Third Quarter Moon   Virgo

River god had downstream sails and
upstream oars moving in his blood.   *Geb was looking up at Sky.*
Sacred siblings brought their staffs for the task
of guarding mounds.

Ants cardinally dispersed from hills,   *as diversion*
when quake and current joined,
took their places.

A grain-scepter thrives
on ground arid, windswept-dry.
Stalk comes down at snake holes' rim.
So there, elevated by a green fist,
lands again.

In rhythmic
percussion, a cooperation sound, Earth
and River keep mound snakes where they
should be:
in the ground.

Full Moon   Virgo

Sweating tar and last year's cider.
Hand claws repeat the scraping motion.
Finally, light a scavenged cigarette's last end point paper.
Drinking fire, tasting ash, eyes wide with hunger.

Burnt seeds, with their heat condensed
affirm latent vine's lost botanical possibilities:
low-water season veal and chilis.

Simmering caldron reason-formulae,
magic conserved in method, so inherited,
animal's endurance for the warriors
from kinesthetic memory, right through fingers is taken.

See Glossary

Set

Angels, spit-fire

Nefertem

Sobek

Temu

Nut

Set

Maneros

LIBRA

To a window, left open on the night,
Set, red-haired, came unnaturally symmetrical.
Features finished off with pockmarks, as usually his way.

The destructive force of desert storms
was in a seeding myrrh bouquet
that he upheld light, bedbug tight, with lettuce-potent greenery.
Set warned me on the dangers of personifying the Sun.

Inevitable confrontations with spit-fire angels.
Challenges to figure-eights – danced against opponent boxers
who, at the critical loop-turns,
resort to abilities of the phoenix – are possible.

Caves, lion-abandoned, wait on mountains to be filled
by what punitive process
go-between mediums to lettuce-green grade flames, order.

Kyil-khor in cigarettes wait to take time's form
on a floor coated incrementally by silence strikes layered upwards
to karmic restructuration.

What of serpent in the soul could forcibly shed its skin,
scarred, burned atomic-degree.

Dawn, Set kissed me,
missed the point we supposed my third eye to be.
Again warned me on the dangers of personifying the Sun.

New Moon

When arrives the Red Lion Rider

machines will defy their makers' intentions,

fights will turn the way of weapons,

enemies will be the least likely of brothers.

Girls left standing with the herds will talk to trees about injustice –

yield of bitter almonds.

Combatants – crowns upper and lower – will bond

once crossed sides over.

Queen will skip automatically over tiles,

when arrives the Red Lion Rider.

First Quarter Moon   Libra

Who from a downstream-perspective watching
listens to the whispering reeds,
first between papyrus fans, feels Ionian breeze.

Then from a downstream perspective ever-watching
at the lull of a motor,
metal dragonfly wings,
hears Nefertem laughter.

At the imitation oasis,
far into date-palm palace shade,
Nefertem, he's laughing
at the scene he sees.

By one artificial pond
a girl is avifauna-painting
the living things she sees.
Watercolors best describe the quality
of the latest genus:
mechanical steel flying birds.

From a downstream-perspective Nile bank,
who listens to the whispering reeds
can learn how the negative pinwheel spaces
between papyrus fans
are filled by opposite-direction
warm sea breeze.

Between fans and reeds on the current,
chlorophyll-crown light's laughter
is incoming by its sinuous way.

Half Moon   Libra

Fall-time aspiration
to lambada improvise free,
with open snakeskin heels.

All the way from a honey cave with birds,
come westward, Zephyr-carried whispers:
Keep it Real.

Girl in mixed-matched sunset colors
downhill hopscotched
to Ratatat sound at dawn.
Sun sailed out the spray paint way;
neon watched it go.

Night-sky bile acid called in vital iron mineral
from yellow flower Passion herbs.
Dark Ages painting: goddess as Bull Island market maid
waits on patient dandelion chalice rim,
thoughts concealed.
At storm's blink-awake eye center
is cherry red anemone yield.

Sideways writing, saving space
on poppy diary pages,
flexible light letters
wrote their last scarab-dream entry
in a doorway floor journal, on modern-day fantasy.

Third Quarter Moon Libra

Sobek traced out a path
in lifting armor scales rotation.
Bangled crocodile followed it with serpentine intention.

Temu, the setting Sun, was provoked by impending darkness.
Nut fell as Set foresaw: raven wild,
holding an Escher-grid of twisting serpents.

Present in shadows, *kapha*.
Embodiment of sinking sand immersive, absolute
as silt by flooded Nile.

Crocodile bangles collide silent,
jewellery struck, *muladhara*.

The Sun took one step back to charge,
interpreting the desert's words as invitation to combat.
A mouthful of sinking sand, his newfound opponent.

Kingly prayers require from statues reactions-complacent.
Animated inventions are nodding by mechanics.

Full Moon   Libra

Mouse, who from its keyboard

by carving knife is cut.

Rats,

anarchists who hold rallies, peaceful from the wall.

Rain that gives black eyes

by punching out kohl.

Land patterns: maps

made by twisting stocks in fields of corn.

Footprints on Mountain faces

left by an escapist version of wild shadow-man.

Harp players, captured over in advance of peace-declared,

this by engraving stelae

with narcissistic victory-plans.

Tyrants are known to suffer the heat.

Crescent horseshoe-silver

and elephant:

strategies that collide in molten logic.

Strings plucked by moths strayed from a plague,

Maneros,

rise and fall.

See Glossary

Bennu

Sekhmet

Temu

Punt

Nekhebit

Mut

Bastet

Left Eye Aster

Djed

SCORPIO

Last palette of fermenting ambers,
orchard's own warm colors that it scrapped
from the confines of its possibility
before it hit peat,
and gave up its colors in a final yield of persimmons.
Fruit rotating full shadow on twig,
deciding to be still edible.

The apprehensive dawn,
with its oaks all standing in a wood at council,
waits, as rye-whiskey patient,
to be infused with bark's amber essence.

New Moon Scorpio

The merchant who, to his brigand's box
had only three harmonicas.

Outcast is proceeding on:
Walking Saint wayfarer with his lonely drum.
At villages, against percussion, translating for those listening.
Then back to Open Sky,
forging lonely drummer's road, still speaking
what desert rose crystals say.

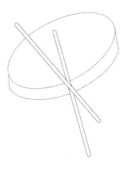

First Quarter Moon   Scorpio

Up from the shoreline and its mountains,
was a home for rays of light.
Fire sky warmth
and its pinwheel: revolving axes flames.
Round they go and nearer:
tones of straw, gold, twig, flax, and clear.

Armada, boat-oar on to the incense trees,
Sun warmth had said to the priests.

Green flame sparkler, the soul bird's tail
was fast and fierce in flight.
Along the skyway, down, wings cut fast the air.
Bennu saw Egypt's first memories below.

There were metal mines,
ruby dusk skies, and myrrh trees.
There were stilt houses with some caged songbirds,
cattle herds, and leopards.
There was Sekhmet, when she was a lion.

Homecoming on sure crystal sea by Temu-tinted waves,
Queen's soul-mission fleet now horizon-checks,
sees Punt,
gods' old land:
the nearing shore.

Half Moon

The Earth is blue, like an orange –
or so they say that it will seem.

Candles from the wick upside-down burning,
knights over checkered tiles by telepathic motion going.
Swan wings upturn, winning from the balcony
a leaning-in reaction.
Lettered specters quoting Miro's cricket,
graveyard offering of cognac.

Tables with their legs are walking.
Chairs hold down the rhythm sound:
music for their game.

Half Moon   Scorpio

On the mirror-lake, glass decoration,
that's where you keep a black swan flock,
trained to sing jokes from comedy operetta.
Though gathered, they tend to revert to their bird dark stuff:
a great grandfather's commissioned tragics.

In the woodland sanctuary,
curtained by symmetrical sheets: the granite-yellow quarries,
a herd of doe is yours, for the enclosed chasing.

The pacing pheasant gestures its premonitions.
One leg up-bent, freestyles its sun-speak,
from intuition-solar on what New Day meant.
Only mechanics to the red-eyed bird's divination
no king can patent.

Fireflies dance a Zecchin night's clearing.
Frame third-act stage, sprigs of red berries.
News from high-view points they're star-interpreting.

Someone, on your invitation, is foot-tapping:
disrespecting the blooming orchard's faeries,
peasant-soul footprints, untraceable-indenting.

In a tight fan, I'm holding my cards:
the Horse, the Empress, another Knight come riding.
Slipped the Joker by the Talking Cat
and let clown inform philosopher, reporting at a whisper.

Third Quarter Moon   Scorpio

A dot bright, a sphere in molded fire-Altamira
steady-hypnotic in its subtle bounces, ellipticals air-track 'round.

Nekhebit, guided by her vulture's thinker-senses,
one wing out, the light, neo-Mut pursues it.

Gravity shifts track's impartial center,
tilts seesaw drift-wood, teeter-totter.

Scavenger-complacent follows avian when the
trajectory she flies is copied over, next elliptical falsified.

Nekhebit, as a vulture
delivers reason by pungent strophe-phases,
one for each season.

Burnt rot is of a sepia quality.
Sprout-grain seeds ferment dark fashion.

Khem by and by to distillation,
formula steady in Grecian rhythm,
Neo-Mut conveys method, circling.

Third Quarter Moon   Scorpio

Yeast: add to river that mystery curse steams to point of boiling.
Home: warm in the dark where jute-corn's soaking.
Topsoil mellow: rinse out Ceres sprouts and roots, innocence-yellow.
Those are hatchlings gone to seed on a conveyor belt of grain-canaries.

Round the days airlocked, starch goes to adhesive sugar.
Five night-crescents, clearing by the Dog Star's watch.
To the brim, still bubbles gather. Gauge the water.
Ethanol, halfway to replacing form of sugar.

Malt of rye and of barley: steam this foul cornucopia.
Temperature: be rising incrementally.
'Round the hours watch your reasoning, logos waxing.
Add for yeast three spoons, at degrees cool one and twenty.

Fractured feathers that conveyor-belt-canaries molted-mellow,
struggle to gain the wash, to make it through the cheesecloth.
Hear copper-echoes going far-star bound as soundwaves.
Tree bark scents the water, Oak seals cracks, absorbing boundaries.

Third Quarter Moon   Scorpio

Distillation brings in swans to the liquid surface.
On instruction from an alchemical manual, through loons they channel,
swans send out their senses on extension-primary feathers,
so converse with their maker.

Aromatic mist appetizes feather-secondaries.
One wing up, they sail as Nekhebit's envoys.
What choreography-avian forms on mirror-lakes in Heaven?
Alchemy is given over to the Oak tree.

The first batch head is for a show,
from the tap: toxic, hook-tongued as Bastet.
Goodnight Left Eye Aster, wait to say it.
Test the heat to goodnight-discard the tail.

What tree, bare, what monkey puzzle with djed-branches
gives to still amber sap?
Watch the glass when you keep the body,
it'll desert-rose-splinter in the eye of chaos.

Full Moon   Scorpio

Pursued to Chimera's Valley.
In the dark, stones aimed at lepers.
Never lost, always leaving,
gray pebble slopes – up and vertigo-falling.
Arriving at dusk for inauguration:
nuclear life forms' night of passion.

Bonfire flips to upright landings.
Acrobats in turn grab horns on head-toss propulsion taurus,
three tambourines rattled to yowls of *taurocatapsia* fans.
Here comes rhino and alpha-rider.

Spinning skirts with strings of beads in circles, learning dances,
watch out for the little ghost – he likes to strangle.
Now they let out the liger.

Sphinx chicks: bad hatchlings, armadillo on a leash.
Throat-burning chemical mead,
taste limestone without the greed.

See Glossary

Nine Nations
Sekhmet
Hathor, Starry Cow

SAGITTARIUS

High sky-river undulates milky pulses mild, that reflect off stars.
Water-light, expansive, unfolds a paper cube, its plans.

Sphinx, sure and regal,
sent out smell on a projectile from her nose-triangle.
With her extension, skimmed the dust off a Zagazig night's edge.

King of nine nations, of arrows therein,
sailed a trajectory cross-sky with marksman's precision.

Tower-hostage soldier
sent out pigeon clawed with love-declaration
to the pharaonic center, with archer's intention.

Now, the harpist who reads aloud
is getting away with your bow. Ink, arrows' poison
will be word that assembles in revolt reader-archers.

An ibis flew through a singular electric zigzag, to capture it all.
Thoth's swiftlet screamed noise on its desperation
that on a screen emitted interruptions in the calm of the beyond.

New Moon   Sagittarius

Courtyard orchard inhabited by a serpent.

Pears monetized by algorithm

and gifted to allies beyond visible stars by mutable carrier-shadows.

Thorns thrive in vials as cultivated swords,

monarchy on Mars.

Plucking petals by couplet incantation, superstition,

letters into paper boats folded,

oaths taken, never forgotten.

Stone tower insinuated with distant wild-herb impressions

called Saint Rita's roses and Mary.

Resident lady alchemist on prince's celestial conquest departed.

Postcard sent by galactic mail and carried at the speed of shadow;

it was addressed to Hell.

Swing set overgrown with roses now into copper finish wilting,

dormouse finds mushroom shelter.

Moths drawn to sunlight grain, illuminated meadows,

wisteria and wild apples.

Swan turns a fan up from twisting ankles' feathers.

Evidence

Thoth, looked down,
hood up, in introspection
on his own electric possessions.

Scribe, archiver, and inventor
who connected clouds to his Book House structure
and let in fire at the state of vapor.

Thoth suspended out a crescent moon,
that from indigo bush coaxed an armadillo
and tinted lapis lazuli a deeper blue.

Crescent called in peace from the season,
just another celebration.
Curious, one prince, the victor,
thought to look on his reflection.
You're never the same after combat.

Böcklin's serpent spoke before the mirror,
so twice tapped the glass with its pointed tail:
two upheld fingers.
Said, *It's mutable, in the glass, your dynamic reflection.*
Recruited from reeds, he seemed first suckled by Isis.
That was a constant.

Submission

Scarab puts up a fight on voyeuristic watch-in screen.
As sword and knife, it yields translucent wings.
By these weapons, feels its way through material reeling in wrath:
flesh, toxic with fumes and pain.

Beneath a film, aloe,
convulsions inflate upwards-sprawling limbs
when total epidermic burn yields to movement.

By a film, aloe, tyrant in anguish is so restrained.
The spit of a gracious, waxy leaf paints over nerves,
encompassing raw skin
in a one-stroke embrace.

Aloes, by a crescent moon for celebration,
were indifferent to his incantation,
"Sekhmet, Sister,
lick my wounds clean
Madonna Lion."

Half Moon   Sagittarius

Through an empty cabin
went a mobile wrestling match,
going as warm tropic shadows.

Conquistador's wife, waiting 'round
lunar time, slept
with all her jewellery.

Along the wall, wrestlers proceeded
linking in a line
shadow dancers' polarity-armlocks.

Attracted to the wall left damp from their fight, by
a suspended half-moon's light, slinking,
went a worm.
Indentation trail it left pointed
to the east.

Third Quarter Moon   Sagittarius

Up from first ocher shades
to last indigo and violet,
revolving on prism's point.

Pillars subtracted from exponential ground
and divided by room's corners
equals projection alter to display translucent treasure.
Light plays a scale in rays by striking temple air: the organ.

Wishes in old amulets, memories of balance
and the floor plan formula,
were carried far into vertigo: the desert.

There, one day, Isaac, alchemist in penitence perceived,
sunrays dancing on a dot,
still in mimesis of sacred sound,
playing odes at light speed.

Full Moon   Sagittarius

Fool's ☉

Fool is the jester
but with his gold can make it fire.
Here's Thoth down the mirrored hall,
as an ibis-beaked clown, laughing observer.
Watch the sound of what he sees by vision-peripheral.

Pilots, light-luminous, conjoined at wing-tips
deep-soil stepped secrets, through gardens Sicilian.

Hunters let their leopards inland-lead who,
mistaking wings for birds, brought them back an angel.

Pyrite struck accidentally by the juggler.
Starry cow painted red by all the truth of stolen fire.

Lapis lazuli as a record keeper
absorbs through moonlight its data,
to know it all at the level of crystal structure.

Fool goes night-sky walking back the Nile's milky extension-highway.

All those emeralds the Spanish wanted,
when you make it to the Jewel Box,
are good for a lucky round of chicken bone tossing.
Ruby-zag to the pearl-zig,
dice, cat's cradle and divination.

Full Moon

By town's clock the hours stopped.

The lion's stars rose standing

and the stoic seconds watched as minutes gave up turning.

In unison the fishes leapt; stream-water swam for spawning.

From their fins, water-drops overflowed the scale-plates.

Jump-fish magic – active word, was heard by Pan as sea-goat.

Lightning – by even bolts – hit Spring of Faun to surface-water.

In sand-black – volcanic ash – the red ram was spitting fire:

heat – invitation to compete, delivered on solar wind to the Auroras.

Europa feigned to bouquet-glance, acting in diversion,

succeeded in a petal-flip to *taurocatapsia*.

The Centaur hit dim target-dot, got the Lynx by unmatched shot

with precision of a marksman.

See Glossary

Temu

Sha

Bastet

CAPRICORN

Geometric drawings, planned when strings link their soul lines
and commissioned by early Temu the Sun from their shadows
by appealing right to their charcoal essence.

Either could have lead the revolution blueprint for the cycle:
linked extension and inversion steps, a string game dance
or the Sun at early Temu entertainment, who noticed languid
and nodded at the durability of their acrobatics.

New Moon   Capricorn

Looking up from time explained in onyx crystals,

subtly balanced steps ascending,

silhouette of vertebral journal.

To see *2, 3, 5,* and *8*

form a spiral in the land's own matter.

Each shell native to salt and sand

selected and so placed by the land,

sang new moon songs in a tidal choir.

To see how harmony result from organic secret in the numbers,

vibration of steps outlining passage sculpture.

First Quarter Moon   Capricorn

Sha Dog is advancing on,
maintaining speed through distance,
always east two dunes past the trail I've gone.

I did not believe so did not see
that a forked-tailed sha was following me.

I'm traveling-composing as I'm going.
Head-nodding, that is tempo keeping.
Space between us grows ever smaller—us now that there is another
and that around us ever wider.

There's a pull just for hunting,
Sha Dog emits it on prey he's pursuing.
His mother, by the Moon, orchestrates her pastel lasers;
light hits my footprints lunar as Sha Dog tracks me.

I've heard of the prints Sha leaves: real indentations on cracked mud,
when with the sunrise, charging, calls in blood.

With a wire good for containing a bonfire,
I note down ash-sand and sulfur-gravel
line pairs on memories held in what river pebble
hand that holds quill wire hits in the pocket of Sha Dog's nostalgia.

Campfire luminance reaches wide.
At literacy's lights-out, command brave and stoic
to *stay back, Animal.*

Half Moon

Capricorn

Petrified to stone,
when she perched top-marble's crumbled bones,
feathers of a dove far-flown.

Columns grew in poolside rows,
their Corinthian caps held captive birds,
semi-sculpted, protruding from high aviary-marble.
Alternated doves and ravens.

At opposite width-ledges to water's length-confine
were composing-Narcissus and nymph Echo-responding.
Prisoner-birds felt free flight on winds going inter-islands.

Correspondence folded precision-strong,
along lines dotted by dialogue's symmetry   -
to paper boats that carried poems cross-pool as cargo.

Lyrics ballad-advanced pool's surface, dancing,
scale-ascending out to Apollonian rhythm's reaches.
Rope ran rhyming knot-paths through the letters with loops;
turns seal-locked at faith: boat's anchors.

Half Moon   Capricorn

Myrrh trees in vases and tranquil lemons
flanked cedar-woodland's cascades at the fountains.
Pool's ocean-blue tiles tuned to tints for introspection
the blood to hill-grove's circulation.

Round walls secluding cavern's sacrality,
blue lichens paraded their lions as warm light.
Before gates' entrance stood wild Ishtar's apricot.

Mountain-deep there's a room, temple-adjacent:
therein a priestess received antiquity's tyrant
and incense guided their psychosis. Inhaled Aurora,
from myrrh-root up to crown-cone smolder.

Narcissus and Echo-maledicted
found palace-cavern's pristine acoustics –
lines chosen random from Vivaldi.
In sight was sovereign's hunting-sanctuary.

Brim-Gallé touched with signature pollen mark-lips
and Ishtar released blossom's distilled essence,
when tree's fruit rotted-amber in a playland of opulent lapis.

Half Moon   Capricorn

Then picked up camp the gypsie pair.

Echo transposed their song, harp parts and all,

three octaves West off quartz wall,

on hearing the Company was returning to mine the quarry.

Paths deer-indentured were softly walked.

Crusade to stray far-feral, on the steps of artiodactyls.

Sacred mission, pilgrimage without a destination.

Stings low-tuned,

tranquil palms at the sand bar, Echo has gone, now deeper the song.

Through cracks Shu leaves, sunrise directs in apparitions

and releases stray stars – fire shards to crown them with comet-halos.

Bastet sent three leopard cubs, up, to Hermit's Cave.

Cubs found him,

as a lotus-held flame, untouchable, in visualization-crystal

and coughed up jewels.

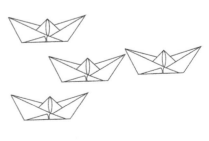

Third Quarter Moon   Capricorn

Shadow-stepping doe, shifting in from beyond the trees, so walked
the created.
Watchers proceeded in split-hoof dust,
going shadow-shifting too.

Kind signal validation for watcher-celebrants
going in procession with their cedar staffs,
a squirrel as ocher smeared in light-refracting shades
ran across
their anticipated path.

Limes and lavender vibrated, so were framed, selected
by the hour of Pan enclosure
when the herder, upon waking, by old habit
scanned the sky.

By the rooster's watch, fields went to seed.
To standing fawn and playmate doe,
it was the one-eyed ram who told them what to do.

Single gaida note sustained,
drew in on sunlight a trapper's tale
from a minute marshland painting,
witnessed by four obedient cardinal watcher-winds.

Full Moon   Capricorn

Wolf let lapse distance from the pack he travelled behind.

A thousand schoeni, desert-hours times hitchhiking-speed,

past the last stone marking open lawless plane.

One of Bastet's vagrant kitties, atomic margins also claimed.

Wandering soul-siblings met, inevitably.

Stepped in tango-resemblance,

Chacarera-mimesis to flat rock mesa floor for dancing.

Recited dialogue, script cast back-to-back.

Strand of lama hair crosses the other over like a sail,

two stray ends intertwining words in threads.

Sunlight came as yellow dawn, curtain to a bed, the rocks.

Two cairn figures, permanent and strong,

balanced at hilltop mesa holding hands.

Moment to see as a sphere, the Sun.

See Glossary

Nut

Khem

Leopard

Nephthys

Ma'at

AQUARIUS

The key concluded its rotation.
Once notice had come to town's Printed Sun
that Berlin was over, they'd release me.

There's a wind-swept cabin on isolated face of bare mountain
that I'd furnish with some illegal stills.
Time, the epagomenal kind, showed me a good turn.

Electricity is in the hands of who remembers
Nut's storm-belt, in its home-up, before the wires.

Decanted lightning from the milk pitcher:
Vermeer's model.

Electric bolts ripped a white sail through:
triangle gone fishing the North Sea.

Pearl divers sent their signals:
static, white noise, chaos, source-TV.

Miracles are when the spark components of phenomena
cooperate from the inside in mutation,
performing a variant, singular and unrehearsed:
their revolution's vision.

New Moon

Attic dust affected by zephyr-tinted light.
The current new moon
entered for data
collected when
in beams it landed
on activity concealed therein.

Tinted by one stroke, that
fell and
rose again, Merilyn:
guppy lips were painted over
sanguine
Khem red.

Goldfisch-Weib, the guppy-lipped was asked to set their story
on Celestial Waters, Nut
and asked to take through half-closed
lotus buds, a Spanish evening walk.

Solar eclipse when the Earth looked down
at pretrial in the box and
the Moon in
its omnipotence
went
to report back to the Sun.

First Quarter Moon   Aquarius

Standing figures, character stones, left as sculptures all alone.
At sunrise they will be telling fables and romanticising scarabs.
Comets, to open desert directed home.

Pharaohs, who by night receive in mystic meeting
galactic strangers, come with carved moonstone pegs
and stardust tents.

Venice of Mark's chimeric feline and Singapore's legendary lion
make believe their way to Heaven.
Paws up on the Jewel Box, bipedal and solemn,
sky-pride waits for sovereigns, wings folded at council.

Moonstone, the negative shards
resulted from carving tent peg tops
into imitations of illusion-clouds.
No pages left in this journal for recording shooting stars.

In infrared delusion, dreamt
that the attic door, from the inside, opened.
The specter now, is in control.

Half Moon

Aquarius

Cold love cuts off precise –
a clean line.
Lightning's orders came in dot-pixel colors:
Skip rocks with rose quartz crystals.

That's how ancient stone riverside
got its concentric land-map circles:
by a topographical ripple
on a captive piece of green river
and its keeper, the wells and tiles.

Silicon records memorize the domestic papyrus first,
it's at mandala's dot-point center.
Then quiet quartz crystals, as they outwards-slinkey,
absorb the outer rings.

Pool's surface tranquil, marked by moment's lightning.
From tiled depth, up, came a golden fish to breathe.
It snapped mouth open, as a whale.

Spirit spoke from electric-night's dot-colors,
said, *Cast down your nets.*
That was instruction of Luke's color by number.
So was the ephemeral circle map on surface-water
cast by freedom's wayward hand, disaffected in frustration.

Half Moon   Aquarius

Beyond the pool and the ripples

left by rose quartz crystals,

artisan before the guild window, arms open,

releases his work.

They've finally invented mechanical scarabs.

Wings work, so fly and orient

by water-map expanding circles.

While Pharaoh, power's chieftain,

meets with far-sky sailors.

Third Quarter Moon   Aquarius

Underfoot, sand-breath upward-standing elevates me.
I triangle on the river-slit dark ground
until Spirit moves when it smells decay
and West Bank orients me.

There's the Hall of Truth. See what it is like there.
Star puppets feel out equilibrium on strings
and reach the fixed sensory turn-points.

Convicted cat with his spotless pelt,
still unblemished back, with his leopard limbs outspread
clings to a granite grave door limit. Inhales, anticipating
tombstone vengeance. Here's Nephthys' son.

Mobile of astral ornaments lets down metal cut-outs
according to the generated scar-stain spots.
Sky fire points appear in real time to circles, pelt-deep burnt,
that go expanding exponentially in clusters out.

How did the leopard get its spots?
Lookout jackals, mountain mesa-perched at dusk,
perceived it all in one head-turn, diagonal-slanting glance.

Full Moon   Aquarius

Pipes, method still hot with aromatic embers,
hearths to cerebral domus.
The initial point for departure past fly lights,
far into starry kite Crux reason.

Between profane gingerbread tree *häuser*,
they exchanged paper planes
delivered by postal stamp grade parrots.

Parrot-delivered paper plane,
received when silent Macaw wings
feigned to alight by candy-roof, top-cage,
blue downfolded indigo silent.

Merchants' boats left to mangroves,
walls-bamboo below eclipse red and quiet.
Plane's top paper layer
scabs its grainy criss-cross in pieces.

Anthropomorphic smoke-stands twisted.
Ascension dances in duet left fermented breadfruit far below,
when they came upon the Jewel Box.

Hermes, with butterfly-swimmer's mechanical Ma'at-wings,
headed from the Aegean
to a view-point in the Mediterranean.
And treaded wing-circles counter-wave
to watch smoke-strands dance the sky.

See Glossary

Punt
Ma'at
Tefnut

PISCES

There are playful far-strayed angels
gone shadow-catching to high-hedge mazes.

Nest origins release their incubated contents,
stacked in a second origin cave.
To soil-velvet from alcoves on honey walls, swiftlets rhythmic-fall.

Leopard cats arrived at a Venetian island by way of the Lagoon,
swimming silent in formation as one grotesque canal monster.
Their shape-shifter descendants inhabit still the Castle.

From the rough boat park,
on wind salt their silence sharp is felt as bitter nettles.

New Moon Pisces

Stray rambler takes dream-refuge

at a graveyard out past Nile City on the outskirts,

nameless fetal-pose figure, she-hermit.

Suppressing its essence

from signals echoed through visions-unconscious,

Albino Lion gives statutory presence

to an unmarked grave.

Narcolepsy afflicts who accepts absolutely

autonomous defense as safety.

First Quarter Moon   Pisces

Out in Guild's margins, they're always chasing
Painter Saint who with each canvas – Christ-capture succeeded –
will prigger-predictably be up-departing.

All Artists' Keeper lives by plunder. Rich his works, this jackroller.
From graffiti site, he's first to flee, leaves his friends – may they be.

Sky will have the depth of glass-enamel,
when you turn yourself in, to the personified Sun, for execution:
Finish me off, I just won't make it.

Here's a conch shell on the floor of this free-standing cell.
Floor-sand has supported old the weight
of flood-time Lower-Lands id Sea.

Into the corner, Fibonacci's spiral is thrown.
With no memories of a Phoenician childhood,
no one can hear the ocean.

Sad *a cappella* sings out numbers, it's Pisan-counting.

82

Aria to Pb

Moving Escher-grid of fins and fish.

Eros sung in fans of light-refracting scales.

Count the fugitives,

just distinguish between the tails.

Now they're undulating sound-escaping,

only as ritual,

making lavender-mind flip-turn circles.

Left Behind Minnow joins two points,

between them latent;

it knows this makes the perfect shape.

Minnow's the last one,

but it knows how to get to Radius End, so it goes.

Once every other second flood,

in memory of the almost-fish,

of breath, wind, and a blade snap-cut reed,

the last minnow swim-flip-turning goes.

Pan's aria for fresh-cut wind-whistle reeds transposed.

Half Moon Pisces

Upstream-circle ceremony downstreams.

New fish-confusion is coming as water-cargo.

Girl in the sun-cooked vase, between cornucopias

of Sapho frayed teardrop-leaves,

listens to fading fog-voices

in one beyond the current choir sing,

We miss the incense trees in Punt.

They brought back vines and lost minnows, some green-haired,

on current-weary beams.

From Libya, they even brought back Poseidon.

Third Quarter Moon   Pisces

Deep ocean dark spiral sepia as red thread.

Endless labyrinth, monument undersea-standing.

Indigo and metallic were its high lost Legend Island walls.

The starting point, a spout that rusted bile blue.

Water lead-pipe circuits gone,

paved the way, by contamination.

Storybook's great fish, now a carcass oil-flaming.

At peak of ice-dust pain,

he wore blue swim fins in the shower,

so backwards-stepped the maze.

Heels descending,

one-two, water-ground touching.

No one as witness to the metronomic kinesthetics

of remembered agony.

Teal corrugated iron cabin and its still sea-raft base,

fixed forever at sterile chaos eye,

the centermost point of a violence-induced storm.

Ancient gull island temples were revisited,

their energies again perceived.

That shiny stone, *marmaros*

copied to parchment in its soul light,

all *sprezzatura*-ease.

Third Quarter Moon   Pisces

That effervescent flying fish,
cold moon-slice shoulder blades.
Against night's high ink waves,
butterfly swims with Ma'at wings.
Goes bamboo raft direction facing,
all *sprezzatura*-ease.

Star Council of four and twenty decided on his fate.
Straw-drew to live the senet game,
two pulled short,
those were the bait.

At the turn around House of Waters
came decisive moment's plank.
Senet sticks cast up the popcorn way,
time of one wave count was their descent.

Electric tide uncertainty,
green velvet table chance,
entertaining jester called Hesitation,
then had his turn to laugh.

Merman on trial in a proton-neutron net.
The lead spout that rusted indigo,
those unforgiving pipes.
Sardines waited on moon-slice shoulders,
dreamt of on-swimming naive *marmaros*,
of a butterfly stroke to a tropic nighttime sea
propelled by strapped-on Ma'at wings.

Third Quarter Moon Pisces

One up, three down.
The senet sticks fell illusion-moon conjunction way.
Bait player danced three houses on.
Come his next turn,
it was game board waltz alchemy.

Jester at the Star Council of four and twenty
turned around,
assumed spontaneous disrupter's authority.

Artificial leap and swim fish turns
were so declared from that point free.
So flew-swam with strength that
surpassed all of fashion's fonts and shortcut keys
and fractured nighttime's high sepia waves
at their incline tops, Solomonic.

So were allowed to coil-spring leap,
those fresh Ma'at flying fish wings
and to trace
Raffaello's *sprezzatura* dust
on wave tops,
all along the tropic lines.

Full Moon   Pisces

Cause

Flies alight
and fold their wings
at the punch bowl's copper rim.
Sea-Monkeys release from citrus rind rings.
Santo grido dell'arme.
Tefnut's roar continues
on in the
memory   *birra, sangria*
of survivor witnesses.

Insides of cups are rusted green.
Empty bathtub on the grass contains
Kiki in her nude-toned bikini.   (Alice)
Ant-parades along ridge clavicles
finally reach honey integuments   (ameba shaped)
on symmetrically mosquito-bitten cheeks.

Head leans on one shoulder, an ostrich egg
hand-placed to incubate in a
vulture's nest.
24 h at the pace the short
hand moves.
Head switches shoulder when it's back at noon.
Twenty-four more epagomenal
hours.

From the nursery section,
cornhusk stares on in her Carila dry leaves.

Influence

On the lawn,
the oak chair from the dining
room table head. Aphrodi-ziac-chi-li-rrred.
Myrrh smolders on
an ashtray. Last scent dies
on matter so challenges
Shu's skeletal structure.

For Shu, with one
ostrich feather
held vertical in his bandana.
Air permanent through epagomenal heat, holds up
the sky,
and columns, when they imitate air,
seem right.

Photographer draws her stare,
with rhythm measured
by perfect calculation,
up a spider thread suspended diagonally from the Celestial West.

Full Moon

A funnel
from a transparent ovoid, drop,   *volume of one cubit*
drip
drops into the receptacle-carafe:
eggshell infusion.
On the chair,
oak,   *Aphrodi-ziac-chi-li-rrred*
by gradual drip-
drop
cup-sips,
Shu performatively drinks the cubit[3].

Lightning moors in written law
when Pip,
kept on the chair by the photographer,   *his idea*
fights to disbelieve delusions
involving low-ranking angel
processions.

Glossary

Aat Sanctuary - In *The Legend of Horus of Behutet and the Winged Disk*, Thoth attributed the sycamore and the acacia to this sanctuary.

Angels, spit - fire angels - Wadjet, the cobra goddess sister of Nekhebit who protects the pharaoh. Wadjet was associated with Upper Egypt and her attribute was the red crown of the pharaoh, whereas Nekhebit also a protector of Upper Egypt was associated with the white crown.

Anubis - The jackal-headed god, sometimes Bastet was a consort.

Anubis, jackal-guide - The jackal-headed god of cemeteries, tombs and death, responsible for embalming the dead and weighing souls was a guide for lost or abandoned children.

Apelle - A painter in ancient Greece whose craft drew live birds to the realistic grapes in his legendary paintings.

Bastet - Bastet was the cat-headed goddess responsible for the performing arts, home remedies, cats, intimacy, fertility, pregnancy, childbirth and children.

Bennu - Bird that represented Ra's soul.

Bull's Graveyard - According to Herodotus, there was a graveyard for domesticated bulls on the outskirts of Heliopolis, city of the Temple of the Sun.

Death of Horus - Seth imprisoned Isis when he murdered Osiris. Thoth helped her escape and suggested that she might birth Osiris' child in secret so that Seth would not murder him to replace Osiris thereby securing rulership of Egypt. At Per-Sui, a town near the Reed Swamp, Isis was denied shelter by a villager whose child was then stung out of vengeance by one of the seven scorpion goddesses accompanying Isis. The goddess of compassion purged the child of scorpion venom by incantation, only to be subsequently informed on the death of her son Horus.

Djed - The djed was a diagram of Osiris' spine with four horizontal crossbars. It was the symbol of structure and stability commonly used in tombs, to ensure stability in the afterlife, by association with Osiris in his role as keeper of the underworld.

Elephantine - The Greek name for Abu, called the City of the Beginning on which the Qerti, the Nile's source openings from which the Milky Way merged into earthly river, were considered to be located.

Elephantine, elephant - According to E. A. Wallis Budge in his translations of Egyptian Texts, 1912, the island's name referred to its shape. Granite as well as precious and semi-precious stone came from Elephantine.

Elephantine, stone - In *The Legend of the God Khnemu and of a Seven Years Famine*, Khnemu, a god who existed on Elephantine made a proposition to the king Neter - khat who had been informed that the Nile had not risen for an extended period of time, resulting in a famine. Nete-khat went to the island's temple and underwent the necessary rites to announce his presence to Khnemu. Khnemu offered to appeal to the Nile God Hapi to rise the river and end the famine. To recognize this act, the king established sacred territorial confines that he attributed to Khnemu with terms of mandatory offering in cuts of grain, game, fish and live stock on the part of the residents of this area. Neter-khat had the new terms for presenting offerings to Khnemu inscribed on a stone stella.

Geb - The Earth god and the brother - husband of Nut.

Grapes - In Egyptian battle narratives, grapes are a metaphor, interchangeable with blood.

Hathor, Starry Cow - Hathor is a massacring agent sent by Ra to disseminate the population of Egypt in the version of the Legend of the Destruction of Mankind as it is written on the walls of a room in the tomb of Seti I at Thebes. A red drawing of a cow with thirteen stars is on the wall facing the door from which this room is entered.

Harpa - Khruti - The infant Horus, son of Isis and Osiris esoterically conceived after Osiris was axe-murdered by Set.

Heru - Behutet - A created work or son of the Sun god Ra (as Ra - Heru - Khuti), generated from Nut, who acts on behalf of his father in battle. Notably in *The Legend of Horus of Behutet and the Winged Disk* by taking the form of a winged disk to pursue the enemies of Ra on the celestial waters.

Heliopolis - The city of the temple of the Sun. Bouquets were left at temples as offerings.

Hu - Hu or Manifesting Incantation accompanied the Sun god Ra on the barge that carried the Sun across the celestial waters with Sia or Perception and Heka or Magic.

Khem - Ancient Egypt was called the land of Khem, meaning the land of fertile alluvium deposited from the Nile on the river's banks.

Khepera – The sun god in his role as the morning Sun and as the creation god.

Leopard - When Set, the god of violence turned into a big cat, Anubis avenged Osiris – who Set had attacked and murdered – by scarring the big cat's pelt with a hot pole. In Ancient Egypt, visible stars were associated with the pelt of a leopard. Set as a leopard wore a map of departed ancestors branded as stars to his back, as punishment at the hand of Anubis – a guide for lost and abandoned children.

Left Eye - The Eye of Horus associated with the Moon. Horus lost his left eye in battle with Set. Thoth, the moon god repaired it and this process is comparable to the waxing of the moon from the time during which it seemingly disappears from the night sky.

Lotus – The lotus was associated with Upper Egypt while the papyrus was associated with Lower Egypt.

Ma'at - A winged form of Isis associated with cosmic balance, order, harmony and consciousness of these principles.

Maneros - The son of Egypt's first king whose premature death is commemorated by Egypt's first hymn. According to Herodotus, the hymn *Maneros* was composed and sung by the Egyptian people in mourning at the time of his death.

Min - The first Pharaoh of Egypt according to Herodotus' consultation with priests at the temple of Hephaestus in Memphis.

Mut- The Matriarchal vulture goddess.

Nefertum - To the ancient Egyptians, the perfection of the lotus flower was an incarnation of the Nile flora god of perfume Nefertum.

Nephthys - Nephtys was the sister of Isis, the two were symbolic complements of each other. Isis was associated with light and Nephtys was connected to darkness and the night. At the death of Horus, Nephthys and the scorpion goddess of medicine Serqet joined Isis in lamentation and suggested that she pray that the Sun Barge make stand-still during its passage through the sky.

Actors hired to weep at funerals were called hawks of Nephthys.

Nekhebit - The vulture goddess derived from the matriarchal goddess Mut. Nekhebit was portrayed flying in profile with one open wing in front of her and the other pointing down. In her role as a vulture, Nekhebit metabolized rot and fermented matter to generate new life.

Nile, Nile fisherman - According to the biographer and historian Jean de Joinville in *Life of Saint Louis*, spices from Eden cumulated in the nets of fisherman on the river Nile.

Nile, low Nile - Hapi, the river god who directed the Nile's rising from the city in the center of the river or Elephantine did not flood the river for seven years, resulting in depleted grain supply described in the *Legend of the God Khnemu and of a Seven Years Famine.*

Nile, transformation by the Nile - In the Contending of Horus and Seth, the two rivals for the rulership of Egypt turn into hippopotamuses to fight in the Nile.

Nine Nations - Nubia was the seat of the nine nations of the bow, conquered by Horus.

Nut - The night sky goddess. Shu as air separates Nut from her brother - husband Geb.

On - The Egyptian name of the city called Heliopolis by the Greeks.

Punt - In Ancient Egypt, Punt was considered the cradle of Egyptian culture and religion before the Old Kingdom. Queen Hatshepsut lead a fleet on a trade mission to Punt Land on divine instruction.

Qebhet - The name of the whole area around the Nile's first cataract.

Qerti - Considering the Nile as an earthly arm of the Celestial Waters, Qerti were the source of the river and the sky waters' limit, compared to breasts in *The Legend of the God Khnemu and of a Seven Years Famine*.

Ra – The sun god in his role as the mid-day Sun.

Sekmet - A lion - headed goddess responsible for justice, biological weapons in warfare and mass immunization from whose breath the desert was said to have been created. Sekmet and the cat - headed goddess, Bastet, responsible for harmony manifesting through sensuality, medicinal remedies and midwifery were originally two aspects of the same goddess.

Serqet - The protective goddess of medicine who acted as an immunizing agent against snake bite and scorpion stings. In her role as a psychologist, Serqet enabled the survival of emotional turmoil. She is depicted in Egyptian art with a scorpion on her head.

Seshet - The goddess responsible for keeping records on pharaonic reigns and land ownership and for the division of territorial confines. She was a patron goddess of scribes and librarians.

Set - The god Set, called Lord of the Desert was the god of storms, chaos, warfare associated with the colour red and the sterility of the desert. When Set was given theological dominion over the desert, temples to this god were built on the outskirts of Egyptian cities. Thoth attributed to Set the name "Stinking Face" for his use of foul language in combat in *The Legend of Heru-Behutet and the Winged Disk*.

Seti - The pharaoh Seti I was renowned for worshiping Set.

Sha - The Sha was a mythical jackal-like quadruped with a forked tail associated with the desert god Set.

Sobek - The crocodile-headed god responsible for automatic anatomical and psychological reactions and functions. The ancient Egyptians adorned domestic crocodiles with jewlery.

Tefnut - The lion-headed goddess of atmospheric moisture, precipitation and dew. Tefnut was also responsible for drought.

Temu - The sun god in his role as the setting sun.

Tawaret - The hippo goddess of fertility, who was a consort of Set.

Was - Anubis and Set were represented with this scepter, representing divine dominion and power.